IT WORKS!
Revolution in
Space

Suzanne Barchers

Marshall Cavendish
Benchmark
New York

This edition first published in 2010 in the United States
of America by Marshall Cavendish Benchmark.

Marshall Cavendish Benchmark
99 White Plains Road
Tarrytown, NY 10591
www.marshallcavendish.us

Library of Congress Cataloging-in-Publication Data

Barchers, Suzanne I.
Revolution in space / by Suzanne Barchers.
p. cm. — (It works!)
Summary: "Discusses the history of space exploration, how the technology was developed, and
the science behind it"–Provided by publisher.
Includes bibliographical references and index.
ISBN 978-0-7614-4377-3
1. Outer space–Exploration--History–Juvenile literature.
2. Astronautics–Juvenile literature. I. Title.
TL793.B37 2010
629.4--dc22
2008054365

Cover: Q2AMedia Art Bank
Half Title : Henrik Lehnerer/Shutterstock.
P7: David Tise, Inc./Jupiter Images; P7(inset)t: NASA; P7(inset)c;
Eric Middelkoop /Shutterstock; P11: Bettmann/Corbis; P11(inset): NASA;
P15(inset)cl: Terry Morris/Fotolia; P15(inset)cr: Greenland/Shutterstock; P15(inset)bl:
Dreamstime; P15(inset)br: Shutterstock; P19: NASA; P19(inset)t: Miele Vacuums;
P19(inset)c: Shutterstock; P19(inset)b: Ewa/Shutterstock; P23: Zach Copley; P27: NASA.
Illustrations : Q2AMedia Art Bank

Created by Q2AMedia
Series Editor: Jessica Cohn
Art Director: Sumit Charles
Client Service Manager: Santosh Vasudevan
Project Manager: Shekhar Kapur
Designer: Shilpi Sarkar
Illustrators: Aadil Ahmed, Rishi Bhardwaj,
Kusum Kala, Parwinder Singh and Sanyogita Lal
Photo research: Sakshi Saluja

Printed in Malaysia

1 3 5 6 4 2

Contents

Rockets' Red Glare

Pop! *Ssss! BOOM!* Have you ever watched fireworks explode in a night sky? The Chinese invented fireworks and rockets. They were using rockets more than a thousand years ago. The first rockets were used as toys. Hundreds of years later, people started thinking about rockets in a new way. They wondered if rockets could be made into weapons.

Sir William Congreve was a British inventor. One of his projects was turning rockets into weapons. He made the rockets used by the British against the United States in the War of 1812. The explosions from the Congreve rockets didn't do much damage. They did, however, inspire a famous U.S. song. Francis Scott Key, an American poet, watched an attack on a U.S. fort in Baltimore, Maryland. As the bombs were "bursting in air," he saw an American flag flying against "the rockets' red glare." Key then wrote the words for "The Star-Spangled Banner," the U.S. national anthem. Congreve did not count on that development!

Meet Sir William Congreve

William Congreve was born in 1772. He loved rockets and fireworks. When he was a young man, soldiers in India used rockets to fight the British. These **rocketeers** launched five thousand rockets in one battle. That scared the British soldiers. Congreve studied the Indian rockets and worked to improve them. His new rockets traveled farther than the old ones did. He needed money to keep working on them, however. He invited the British prime minister and other officials to see the rockets in action. He launched his rockets from a boat—and got the money he needed.

My improved rocket weighs 32 pounds (15 kilograms). It holds plenty of gunpowder.

The rocket needs to fly almost 2 miles (3 kilometers). It has to be fired from a ship.

The head of the rocket needs to be held by a frame.

Let's hope this frame works!

Balloon Launch

masking tape

5 feet (1½ meters) of string

drinking straw

long, thin balloon

spring clothespin or
strong binder clip

two helpers

1 Thread the string through the straw.

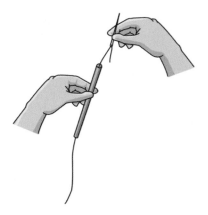

2 Blow up the balloon. Hold it closed with the clothespin or clip. Tape the straw along the long side of the balloon.

3 Stretch the string tightly between two people. Move the balloon carefully to one end of the string.

4 Release the clothespin or clip. How far does the balloon travel? Repeat with varying amounts of air blown into the balloon.

WHO WOULD HAVE THOUGHT?

Homemade Rockets

Rocketry has a big role in history. Rockets started as toys. About a thousand years later, they were used as weapons. Now we send rockets to space. Rocketry is also a popular hobby. Would you like to become a rocketeer? You can join the National Association of Rocketry when you are in middle or high school. Then join a team and compete in the Team America Challenge. Here's the challenge. Fly your team's rocket for 45 seconds. Make sure it reaches a height of 750 feet (229 m). Just make sure the **payload** gets back safely. The payload? One large raw egg!

Space launches are big events.

Rockets help planes fly farther faster.

People build rockets like this at home.

7

Give It a Boost

Do you a have good idea for an invention? Good ideas often occur to more than one person at the same time. That happened with rockets. Sending rockets into space requires a lot of force. That force requires a lot of fuel. Getting to space seemed impossible when people were using gunpowder, because gunpowder is heavy. Then several inventors found ways around the problem.

Robert Goddard was an American scientist. He knew that firing a rifle causes recoil. The gun flies back, or recoils, when you fire it. Goddard wondered if the force of recoil could help launch a rocket. He also thought about using liquid fuel, which is lighter than gunpowder. In addition, he had the idea of dividing the rocket into sections. Each section would carry fuel. The sections could be fired in **stages** and be dropped off when their job was done.

About the same time, two other scientists decided **liquid propellant** was the answer. One lived in Germany. The other lived in Russia. They had never met!

Meet Robert Goddard

Robert Goddard, born in 1882, was sickly as a child. He fell behind in school, but he loved to read. When he was sixteen, he read H. G. Wells's *War of the Worlds*. It was about a Martian invasion of Earth. In 1899, he climbed into a tree to cut dead limbs and started daydreaming about that book. He thought about space travel. What would a space machine look like? He said his life was never the same after that day. He was on his way to becoming a great rocket scientist.

IMAGINE!

Gunpowder is too heavy. The rocket will never escape Earth's gravity.

Liquid propellant doesn't weigh as much, but the rocket would still have to be huge. What if two sections were stacked on top of each other?

Put the bigger one at the bottom. The big part can drop off after the rocket has been lifted far enough.

The next section can take over. There is less gravity by then. Less force is needed. This can work!

Make a Fizzy Rocket

empty film canister with a lid

Alka-Seltzer tablet

water

towels for cleanup

 1 Fill the film canister halfway with water. Place the Alka-Seltzer tablet in the water.

 2 Fit the lid on the canister, making sure the seal is tight. Turn the canister upside down and place it on a flat surface.

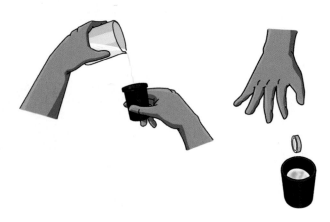

 3 Move away at least 10 feet (3 m) and wait. You'll have to clean up!

 4 Repeat with different levels of water. How does this change the reaction time? How does it change the distance traveled?

Controlled Launch

Robert Goddard's first successful flight with a liquid-propellant rocket was on March 16, 1926. It flew for two and a half seconds and climbed 41 feet (12½ m). When it came down, it landed in a cabbage patch. Now there are missiles that can travel more than three thousand miles. Some have a built-in **guidance system**. Some are guided by a **controller** on the ground. The simple rocket has become a complicated weapon.

The bottom parts of a rocket fall off after firing.

Race to Space

By World War II, rockets were commonplace weapons. The Germans developed the V-2 rocket. This missile could travel about 200 miles (322 km). The deadly V-2 killed thousands of people during the war.

Soon after the war, rockets took on new meaning. In 1957, a rocket made it into space. The Soviet Union, as Russia was called then, launched a radio **satellite**. It was called *Sputnik 1*. The satellite was the size of a beach ball. It went into **orbit** around Earth for three months. It sent radio signals to Earth for twenty-two days. The next month, the Soviet Union launched *Sputnik 2*. It was much larger. It carried a dog.

Sergei Korolev was the talent behind *Sputnik*. He launched the satellite using the R-7 rocket. The R-7 was his country's first **intercontinental ballistic missile**, or **ICBM**. The Soviet Union was in a race with the United States to see who could be first in space.

Meet Sergei P. Korolev

Sergei Korolev was born in 1906. As a boy, he went to an air show and fell in love with flight. He decided to join a glider club to learn more about aviation. He studied hard for many years. By the age of thirty-two, he was a fine scientist. That's when the Soviet government accused him of not working hard enough for his country. He was sent to a labor camp in Siberia. A year later, he was allowed to work in a prison camp for scientists. He studied rockets. He was released in 1944. By the time he died in 1966, Korolev was considered a hero for his work on spaceflight.

YOU CAN'T LOCK UP THOUGHT!

We need more power to get past Earth's gravitational pull. How can we do that?

Let's try a **cluster approach**. We'll use four **boosters**. Everything needs to be streamlined. So we'll taper the boosters.

The boosters will provide enough power for liftoff.

Now all we have to do is make sure it works!

Around the World

beanbag

2 yards (2 m) or
so of sturdy rope

small bucket

water

1 Stand outside with plenty of space around you. Make sure no one is standing nearby.

2 Tie the rope around the beanbag.

3 Spin the beanbag over your head. You are acting like Earth, with its gravitational pull. Spin faster and then release the rope with the beanbag. Watch the path it takes.

4 Tie the rope to the bucket handle. Fill the bucket halfway with water. Now, spin the bucket and think of the forces at work. The slower you spin, the more water spills! Caution: Do not release the bucket while spinning!

WHO WOULD HAVE THOUGHT?

Satellites in Action

Sputnik was the first satellite to orbit Earth. It weighed almost 184 pounds (83 kg). Before then, life went on without the help of satellites orbiting Earth. No one missed them. Why would they? Now we all rely on satellites for many things. Our cell phones and our Internet service rely on satellites. Radio and television broadcasts are sent by satellite. What would we do without these helpful satellites in space?

To the Moon

President John F. Kennedy gave Congress a bold message in May 1961. He challenged the nation to send a human being to the Moon by the end of the decade. That was a tall order! The top rocket scientists in the world went to work on the project. They included Wernher von Braun. Born in Germany, von Braun had worked with the Nazis during World War II. After the war, he moved to the United States, bringing five hundred top scientists with him. The United States wanted the help of these former enemies. The United States was fighting the Cold War with the Soviet Union. The Cold War was a war that stopped short of open battle. It was a competition to lead the world.

Von Braun's new rockets were known as the *Saturn* family of rockets. Von Braun and his team worked for several years on them. The scientists ran the Apollo space program, which sent astronauts to the Moon. In 1969, astronaut Neil Armstrong was first to step onto the Moon's surface. He said, "That's one small step for man . . . one giant leap for mankind." Von Braun helped us make that leap.

Meet Wernher von Braun

You might think a great scientist would be good in physics and math. Wernher von Braun, born in 1912, didn't start out that way. He was a kid who just loved to read. He especially liked reading about outer space. Like Robert Goddard, he read H. G. Wells's *War of the Worlds*. He read a lot, but one book, written by Hermann Oberth, changed his life forever. Oberth was a rocket scientist. When von Braun read Oberth's book, he wanted to become a rocket scientist, too. Do you know what that meant? It was time to study physics and math!

WERNHER!

The *Saturn V* will get three astronauts to the Moon.

The **lunar module** has a guidance system for landing on the Moon.

It can make a soft landing, and we know how to get it back to the main ship.

How will we get the astronauts safely back to Earth? They will need to land in the ocean. I know! We'll have a parachute!

Moon Craters

flour

9 x 13 inch
(23 x 33 cm)
baking pan

round cake pan
of any size

cookie baking sheet

variety of small objects,
such as pennies, marbles,
toy animals, toy trucks

1 Pour flour into each pan. To model an **asteroid's** hitting the Moon, drop a marble into the flour. Lift the marble out carefully. Remember that there is no wind or air on the Moon. Anything that disturbs the surface has a lasting effect!

2 Try making an image of the "man in the Moon" in the round pan, using your objects.

3 There is little gravity on the Moon. If you weigh 100 pounds (45 kg) on Earth, you'll weigh just 16.6 pounds (8 kg) on the Moon. So vehicles weigh less on the Moon, too. Drive the toy truck lightly across the flour. How does it look?

4 Shake your pans and start all over with more objects.

18

WHO WOULD HAVE THOUGHT?

Ideas from Space

Do you think you have any space age inventions in your house? Just look around. Power tools were used to help the astronauts drill for Moon samples. Power tools led to the cordless vacuum cleaner. Do you ski or snowboard? The battery-operated heater that fits into your gloves or boots was adapted from the Apollo spacesuits. You can thank scientists when you play video games as well. Joysticks are like the controller used on the Apollo **Lunar Roving Vehicle (LRV)**.

cordless vacuum cleaner

cordless drill

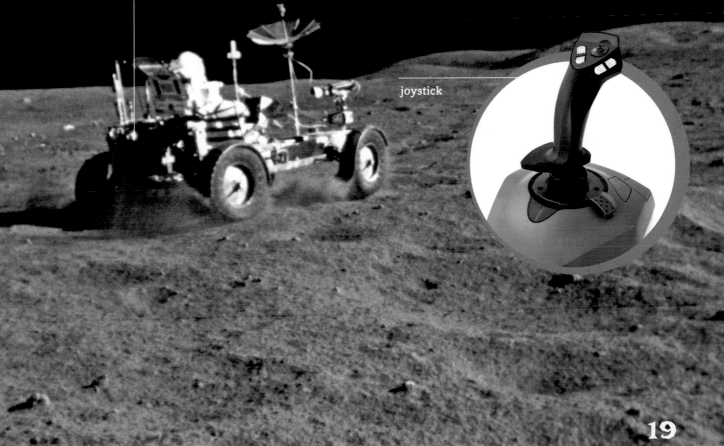

Apollo LRV

joystick

Packing for Space

The first astronauts who worked outside **space shuttles** had to stay attached to the shuttles. They did that with tethers, or ropes. Science fiction writers dreamed that people would one day move freely in space. So did scientists and astronauts. They came up with the **Manned Maneuvering Unit**, or **MMU**.

Bruce McCandless II was a talented scientist as well as an astronaut. He joined NASA in 1966. He was part of the science team that worked on the ground during flights to the Moon. One of his projects was to help develop the MMU. During the time that McCandless worked at NASA, he dreamed of flying into space himself. Eighteen years went by. When he was forty-six years old, he got his chance. He was the first person to use the MMU in space.

Meet Bruce McCandless II

Bruce McCandless II was born in 1937. He loved to go bird watching. He was sometimes teased for his strong interest in birds. His hobby turned out to be useful, however, when he was working for NASA. A new runway was built at the Kennedy Space Center. It was right in the middle of a bird refuge. There was always the chance that birds could fly into a jet's engines. That could cause a crash! McCandless studied the birds nesting near the runway at the space center. He made sure that pilots learned how to avoid the birds.

WATCH THE BIRDIE!

The MMU has to have a guidance system, a warning system, and its own radio.

It will need room for water and oxygen. There will have to be backup systems, too.

It must be easy to control.

A backpack will work! An astronaut will be able fly alone for six hours.

Just How Tall Are You?

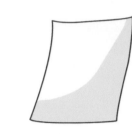

yardstick, meterstick, or measuring tape

blank piece of notebook paper

masking tape

pencil

wall

helper

---

1 Tape the piece of paper to the wall. Place it so the middle is as high as the top of your head. Just before you go to bed, have your helper mark your height on the paper. Measure that mark from the floor. Add the date and put *p.m.* (for evening) next to that measurement.

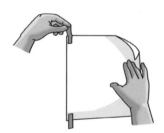

2 Have your helper measure you again the next morning when you first wake up. Add the date and *a.m.* (for morning). You will likely be half an inch (1 cm) or so taller in the morning than you were at night.

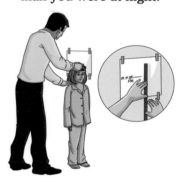

---

3 Repeat this experiment for a few days in a row. What is the average height difference?

4 What is the reason for your change in height? The Earth's gravitational pull makes you shorter during the day. Astronauts can "grow" up to 2 inches (5 cm) per day because there is no gravity in space.

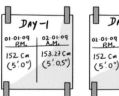

DAY-1

01-01-09 P.M.	02-01-09 A.M.
152 cm (5′0″)	153.27 cm (5′0.5″)

DAY-2

02-01-09 P.M.	02-01-09 A.M.
152 cm (5′0″)	153.78 cm (5′0.7″)

DAY-3

03-01-09 P.M.	02-01-09 A.M.
152 cm (5′0″)	153.52 cm (5′0.6″)

WHO WOULD HAVE THOUGHT?

Everyday Robots

After several MMU flights to repair the space shuttle, people at NASA decided to try something new. They built a **robotic manipulator arm**. The arm could do repairs and work on the space shuttle. That robotics project led to devices such as a voice-controlled wheelchair. The wheelchair can respond to thirty-five one-word voice commands. Scientists also learned how to make robots that can climb stairs and search buildings. The military sent robots like that to Afghanistan and Iraq. The robots helped U.S. troops clear out enemy soldiers from caves and buildings. The robots can do amazing things. They can even find ways to walk across minefields safely.

This robot searches for explosives and destroys them.

Forward to the Future

People have gone to the Moon and beyond. Ice has been discovered on Mars. What might be next? In the past, scientists have gotten their ideas from science fiction writers such as Jules Verne and H. G. Wells. Tomorrow's scientists may dream about Robert L. Forward's ideas. He was a scientist and a storyteller.

Robert Forward was known as a **futurist** because he loved to think about the future. He wanted to find a way to travel among the stars. His biggest idea was to use the Sun and **laser beams** for spaceflight. How? He didn't have everything figured out. His imagination helped other people come up with new ideas, though. Now scientists are figuring out ways to make it possible to fly between the stars. Forward also wrote eleven science fiction books. Who knows what his books might inspire during your future!

Beamed Propulsion Concepts

Meet Robert L. Forward

Robert Forward, born in 1932, grew up very poor. That did not stop him from being active in the Boy Scouts. He was only fourteen years old when he went to the Sixth World Jamboree in Moisson, France. He joined more than 24,000 Boy Scouts. His trip was right after World War II. It was a big trip for a teenager! When he got home, people wanted to know how things were in Europe. He got very good at giving speeches. A way with words ran in the family. Robert was able to go to college because his mother won a contest for writing a jingle. She won $5,000 for writing five words! Robert said, "As a writer I have yet to match that payment of a thousand dollars a word."

SCOUT IT OUT!

Light is powerful. When it hits something, it pushes on it slightly.

What's the most powerful source of light? The Sun! So, make a solar sail. Make it big and make it so that light can bounce from it.

The sail can use the power of the Sun's rays to move through space.

To go beyond the reach of the Sun, use lasers! You could ride laser beams all the way to the stars!

25

Bits of the Big Picture

clothes for three days

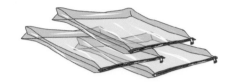

several large plastic storage bags with zippers (if possible, the kind with a system to take the air out)

yardstick or meterstick

 1 Imagine: You need to pack for a weekend in outer space. Everything has to fit into a small backpack, so you don't have much room. Pack your clothes into some of the storage bags. Don't squeeze out the air.

 2 Stack the bags. Measure the height of the stack with the measuring stick.

 3 Let out as much air as possible from each bag. If your bags have no air extraction system, leave a small opening in the zipper area. Then roll each bag tightly and seal it again.

 4 Repeat the measurement. How much space did you save after removing some air? Do the clothes fit? Think about all the details that go into spaceflight!

WHO WOULD HAVE THOUGHT?

Space Technology

Would you like to have a *real* space-age kitchen? You can, thanks to the **International Space Station (ISS)**. The ISS is the biggest structure ever built in space. It has more living space than a typical three-bedroom house. Astronauts on the ISS use a remote command and control system for experiments. That kind of system is now used for a refrigerated oven right here on Earth. You can keep foods cold in it until you are ready to cook them. Then you can use your cell phone, PDA, or Internet connection to start heating up your dinner!

International Space Station.

Timeline

AROUND A.D. 1000
Chinese rockets are used for entertainment.

1792
Rocketeers of India alarm British soldiers.

1804
Sir William Congreve begins work on the rocket that would be named for him.

1812
The British use Congreve's rockets during the War of 1812.

1814
Watching rockets pound a fort in Baltimore, Francis Scott Key writes "The Star-Spangled Banner."

1926
Robert Goddard launches the first liquid-propellant rocket.

1944
Germans use the V-2 rocket to bomb London, England, during World War II.

1961–1991
Robert Forward pioneers developments in spaceflight.

1984
Bruce McCandless uses the Manned Maneuvering Unit to take free flights in space.

1969
Neil Armstrong walks on the Moon.

1961
President John F. Kennedy challenges the nation to send a person to the Moon.

1958
NASA is established by the U.S. government.

1957
Wernher von Braun begins working on a new three-stage rocket.

1957
Sputnik is launched into orbit by the Soviets.

Glossary

asteroid one of thousands of space bodies that orbit the Sun. Some are less an 1 mile (1.6 km) wide. Others are as big as 500 miles (805 km) wide.

booster rocket used to create more push during the stages of a launch.

cluster approach in rocketry, the idea of grouping rockets for a controlled effect.

controller tool that directs the action of a machine.

futurist person who thinks creatively about the future.

guidance system device or group of devices that directs rockets, missiles, or a space vehicle.

Intercontinental Ballistic Missile (ICBM) long-range weapon, capable of flying thousands of miles.

International Space Station (ISS) large facility being built by many nations for research in space.

laser beam a strong, exact kind of light that shines in a very narrow beam.

liquid propellant a lightweight fuel, such as kerosene or liquid hydrogen, used to send rockets into space.

lunar module the part of the Apollo spacecraft that landed on the Moon with the astronauts and later returned them to the main ship, or command module.

Lunar Roving Vehicle (LRV) two-person vehicle used to explore the surface of the Moon.

Manned Maneuvering Unit (MMU) lightweight backpack that allows astronauts to walk freely in space.

orbit curved path of one object around another.

payload cargo on an aircraft.

robotic manipulator arm mechanical arm that can be guided remotely by astronauts to maintain and repair a spacecraft.

rocketeer person who uses or studies rockets.

rocketry science of rockets.

satellite a spacecraft that moves in an orbit around Earth; also, a heavenly body that moves in an orbit around another heavenly body, such as the Moon around Earth.

space shuttle a reusable spacecraft that takes astronauts and equipment to and from Earth and satellites.

stages portions of a launch system that use fuel and then separate from the system.

To Learn More

Books

Space Station Science: Life in Free Fall by Marianne J. Dyson. Scholastic, 1999.

Rocket! How a Toy Launched the Space Age by Richard Maurer. Crown, 1995.

Spaceflight: The Complete Story from Sputnik to Shuttle — and Beyond by Giles Sparrow and Buzz Aldrin. DK Publishing, 2007.

Websites

Take a look at a timeline of rocketry provided by NASA.
http://history.msfc.nasa.gov/rocketry/index.html

To help students and others, NASA's site has in-depth information.
http://www.nasa.gov

Enjoy an autobiography of Robert Forward and related facts.
http://www.robertforward.com/

Index